Inuit Tools

of the Western Arctic

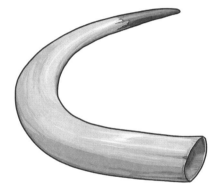

WRITTEN BY

Barbara Olson

ILLUSTRATED BY

Megan Kyak-Monteith

There are many different tools used in the Arctic! Different tools are used for different purposes. Here are some traditional tools that are used in the western part of the Arctic.

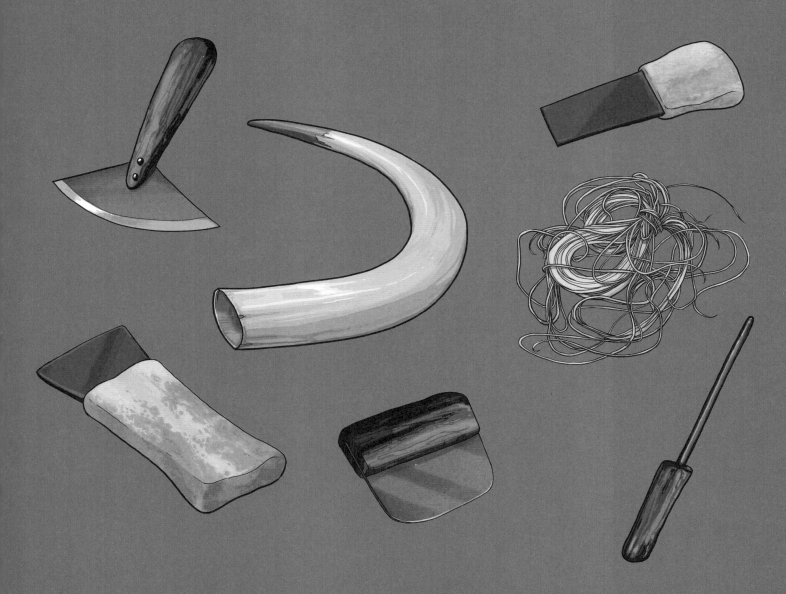

ammiqut
(pronounced UM-meh-qot)

An ammiqut is used for scraping fat off
sealskins. It is made of wood and metal.

qituliqhit
(pronounced qi-to-liq-HIT)

A qituliqhit is a dull scraper used for softening large skins. It is made of muskox bone. It is also called an iqtuqhit.

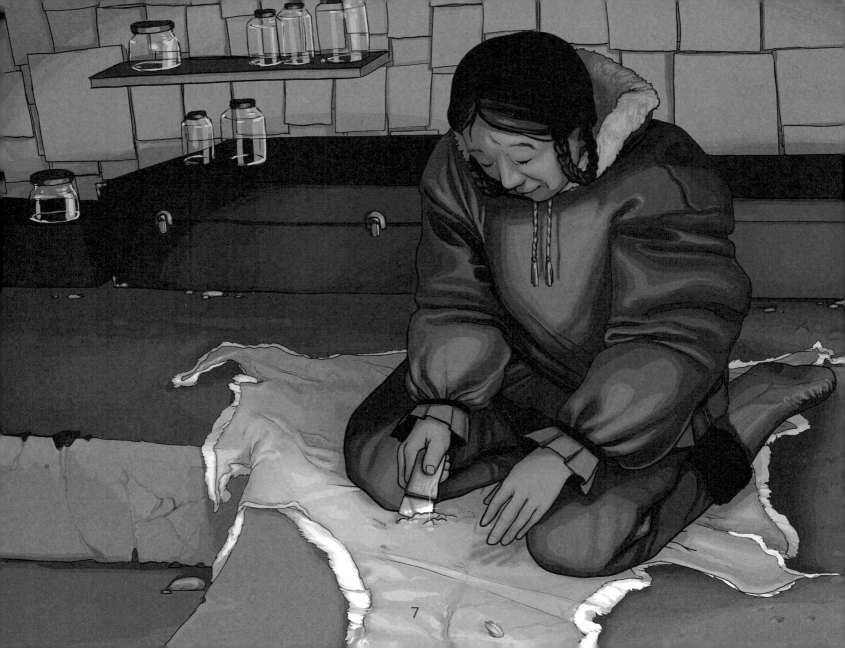

ikuugut
(pronounced i-KOO-goot)

An ikuugut is a dull scraper used for softening small skins. It is made of muskox bone.

kaugaqhit
(pronounced GOW-gaq-hit)

A kaugaqhit is used to pound seal fat for oil. It is made from a muskox horn.

kiliurut
(pronounced KEY-lew-goot)

A kiliurut is used to scrape extra oil off of sealskin as it dries. It is made of wood and metal.

ivaluit
(pronounced EE-vah-loo-it)

Ivaluit are used to stitch together fur or skins for the final piece of clothing. They are made of sinew from a caribou.

ipikhaut
(pronounced EE-pik-hout)

An ipikhaut is used to sharpen all the traditional tools.

Those are some of the tools we use in the western Arctic.
What other tools do you know about?

ammiqut
(UM-meh-qot)

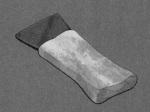

qituliqhit
(qi-to-liq-HIT)

ikuugut
(i-KOO-goot)

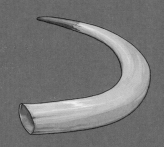

kaugaqhit
(GOW-gaq-hit)

kiliurut
(KEY-lew-goot)

ivaluit
(EE-vah-loo-it)

ipikhaut
(EE-pik-hout)